# Advocacy Plus

# Also by this author

# Advocacy Plus

*A guide for young advocates*

## Nigel Pascoe QC

ISBN: 978-0-244-69233-9

PublishNation
www.publishnation.co.uk

# Introduction

Good advocates build their skills by trying to stand on the shoulders of giants. In my case, first by a fantastic pupillage with Michael King, a marvellous advocate and later Judge on the Western Circuit. A handsome ex-naval officer, blessed with a deep cello voice and all the charm in the world, juries loved him, jokes and all. Most of all, he persuaded, case after case, often in spite of the evidence. I owe him everything. Not least, the love of good stories.

There have been many others. Sir Joseph Moloney QC, austere Leader of my Circuit; John Spokes QC, Head of Chambers and an incomparable cross examiner; and fellow circuit sometime QCs Paul Chadd, Sir Neil Butterfield, David Elfer, David Webster, Michael Hubbard, and Paul Dunkels. I saw Gerald Gardiner QC, and Victor Durand QC. In Court, I marvelled at the skills of George Carmen QC, John Mathew QC, and Gerald Elias QC, the best opponent I have ever had.

So many others. From an earlier generation, preserved on vinyl, Sir Norman, later Lord Birkett QC. Then teachers, notably Eric Crowther, whose own book *Advocacy for the Advocate* remains an excellent aid for young advocates. A good friend to many, not least from overseas.

All of which may help to explain why I wanted to write a different sort of book, anecdotal as well as practical. I willingly plead guilty to thespian tendencies. Advocacy and Acting have much in common, but particularly the need to control respective audiences. It is all about limited concentrated, and sometimes concealed, power. Metaphorically, you wear a fine and attractive coat, but one where you should never see the stitching. Technique concealing art. Some of the material first saw light as a seminar piece or article. I have decided to keep the formats, because it is easier to include and tell stories, which is most of what we do.

My thanks particularly to Sir John Royce, once a fellow leader of the Western Circuit, and everyone else who has helped me, including Her Honour Judge Susan Evans QC, Ian Fenny, Louise Sweet QC, and Sarah Jones.

Finally, I could not have any success worth having without the love and lifelong support of my beloved wife, Elizabeth. We met as students in a Constitutional Lecture and the rest, as they say, is history.


Nigel Pascoe QC
June 2018

# Preface

"Winchester. Murder trial before me. Nigel Pascoe QC prosecuting. From his first sentence, the Jury was gripped. Compelling, structured, fair, utterly devastating. The defendant had no hiding place.

I said at the time it was a model that any young barrister should have heard.

He has always been a most exciting advocate.

He brings to this book an enormous wealth of experience. There are a host of helpful hints. Any aspiring advocate should read and learn from this excellent practical guide."

*Sir John Royce,*
Former Presiding Judge and
Former Leader of the Western Circuit

# Contents

1. Advocacy – an overview      1

2. Public Speaking      7

3. Preparation and Chronologies      9

4. Opening and Closing Speeches      11

5. Examination in Chief and Re-Examination      16

6. Cross Examination      21

7. Prosecution and Defence Advocacy
Tips in Rape cases      25

8. Expert Evidence      36

9. Submissions      44

10. Pleas in Mitigation      45

11. In the Cells      47

12. Advocacy on Appeal      49

13. A Glimpse of Lord Norman Birkett KC      52

14. 'Friends, Romans and countrymen...'      56

15. Reflections      67

About the Author      68

# 1. Advocacy – an overview

The old argument that advocates are born and not made is, I think, a sterile debate. I believe that sensible well-tried techniques can be used to improve everyone who seeks to be a professional advocate. My purpose is to set them down and invite you to practise them.

What exactly is Advocacy?

I like the definition originally attributed to the great Lord Birkett, legendary advocate of the last century. Advocacy is harnessing your own personality in its most attractive form in pursuit of a cause. Please note the emphasis on personality. *Your* personality. If you try to be someone else – by language or expression - it will sound phoney. It is phoney. Television is brilliant at picking out insincerity. So ultimately is the Court room. So be yourself, for better or worse, but always set out be persuasive.

There is an alternative definition which is worth remembering. An advocate is someone who is able to present another person's case better than their own best friend. If you think about it, that means they will have mastered the details of the case better than someone who knows the client exceptionally well. And there is no substitute for meticulous preparation: no short cuts if you really want to persuade.

# Fundamental Principles

So what are the fundamental principles before we consider different aspects of advocacy? I believe there are four, all equally important. First of all, **clarity.** Secondly, **preparation**. Thirdly, **economy and simplicity of language** and lastly, **integrity.**

Let me begin with **Clarity.**

There is no excuse for anyone setting out to persuade judge or jury of the validity of their argument if he or she cannot be heard. I include in that - mumbling, dropping your voice at the end of a sentence and reading badly. It is amazing how many professional advocates have either forgotten or do not bother about clarity of speech. From the very beginning, your first appearance in court, every word must be heard. That pre-supposes some training in speaking in public, but a few simple rules may help.

First you need to conquer those nerves, at least to the point where your throat muscles are not tightening and all that escapes are a few incoherent phrases. So before you speak, imperceptibly for a couple of minutes, make sure you take deep breaths and concentrate on that first sentence, which you will have prepared. Let your hands hang loose at your side or even behind your back. Make a conscious effort to relax. But the best tip to overcome nerves is the comfort that comes from careful preparation.

It might be thought that the best **preparation** is to write everything out in full and simply learn to read it effectively.

Many advocates do just that. Opening a fraud case to a jury requires an absolute mastery of detail and in any event increasingly advocates have to supply openings to the court. But frankly I do not recommend that at the very beginning. The reason is that in most cases it will sound as if you are reading and it will not help you to build up the quick reactions which you need to develop, in order to deal with sudden changes in the evidence or unexpected issues which suddenly arrive.

My advice is to develop initially fairly full **notes**, but leaving gaps. In other words, from the beginning you must force yourself to speak from your notes rather than read a set speech. Incidentally Lord Birkett took that suggestion one stage further. Get into the habit of reducing your fairly full preparation into five key points. Put them on a postcard. Put the postcard in your pocket and you will never need to use it. That is a good tip for short speeches, although difficult for the absolute beginner.

The chances are, however, that you will not be able to use a lectern when you begin. That means you will be looking down at your notes, unless you manage to raise them on an upturned Archbold or Blackstone. It is very important not to mutter into your notes. You must engage with the Court that you are addressing, which of course means that you must look at them as much as possible. It goes without saying that your notes must be readable. Short headings with a black felt tip pen provide an easy answer.

All this raises the **length** of your speeches. When I began, I got into the habit of collecting those sheets of cardboard that sometimes come with new shirts! I wrote on one side and if the speech went beyond that, then it was too long! I suggest your notes, however many pages long, should be written on one of the sides of your blue notebook, so that you can add last-minute thoughts opposite. Then underline key words or phrases.

Think very hard about your opening sentence and even more about the way you are going to finish. So often speeches tail away into anti-climax, often with unnecessary repetition of their better points. It is a sign of second-class advocacy. Your speeches should be surgical: detached, clear, incisive and persuasive. And they should end well.

Now it may be that you are able, almost from the beginning, to speak without notes. That is wonderful and I thoroughly encourage it, providing you have done the preparation beforehand. It is a real gift, it is impressive and it certainly helps to persuade. However the reality is that most of you will want to use some notes, even if later on you have the confidence to do without them.

What about **economy of language**? It is very important, if you want to hold the attention of your audience, that you avoid unnecessary verbiage or repetition. Short sentences. Crisp descriptions. That said, there will be times when a little oratorical flourish is not only useful but positively helpful. And once you know how to mix reason and emotion, then necessarily your speeches will expand.

However that is not good advice for the beginner. You should concentrate when you begin on putting your argument as concisely as possible. Intelligent judges simply turn off when the argument is repeated.

With economy should come **simplicity of language**. Plain unadorned English. That is particularly true of jury advocacy where using an unfamiliar word which may not be understood must be avoided at all costs. The late George Carman Queens Counsel was noted for his straightforward direct speech and incidentally, it is said that no jury speech lasted more than 45 minutes. You should be able to capture your case in that time and retain a jury's attention.

Lastly **Integrity**. Most of us would put this top of the list. To be a good advocate, you must be trusted. That means your tribunal - be they judge or jury - must know that you have not mis-stated any part of your instructions or deliberately concealed fundamental information which you know you should bring out.

Of course, there is a clear distinction between glossing over the more difficult aspects of your submissions and misleading a court. For example, in a plea in mitigation, it is not your duty to put forward every daft suggestion of your client. Many a sex offender actually believes it is important to tell you that the child led him on to assault. It is, of course, utterly wrong, completely irrelevant and counter-productive. That sort of admission against interest can be left in the backsheet and need not see the light of day.

I cannot emphasise how important it is to be straight with the Court at all times. That includes, of course, drawing to the

Court's attention an authority which you has found in your researches, even though it is dead against the fundamental submission which you are making.

And please remember that once you have a reputation for being less than frank with the Court, it will be exceptionally hard to get rid of it. Advocates live in a small world and we get to know those whom we do not trust. You are not going to be one of those.

# 2. Public Speaking

My late father in law, Bryan Walter was the senior partner of Wontners, celebrated solicitors in Broad Court, London, with a lot of independent prosecuting work. A charming and quiet man, with a busy practice, mostly in the Surrey magistrates' courts. One day he took Dorothy, his wife to listen. The verdict was typically uncompromising. 'Bryan, you're mumbling.' Rather than being miffed, he took himself off to a part-time course at the Guildhall of Music and Drama, When I joined the family, he urged me to do the same.

My meeting with a legendary drama teacher, Rona Laurie started on the wrong page. You should realise, she said, that I am terrified. I have never taught a barrister before. I said that if she was frightened, how did she think I felt? Rona laughed and we got on famously.

The lessons included techniques to conquer nerves. Control your voice before you speak by deep surreptitious breaths. Let your hands go limp at your sides or even quietly wring them. Stand up and do not look down at your notes. Do not let your voice drop at the end of a sentence. Watch out for the sibilant S. Tape-record your own early preparation. Allow a good friend to listen to you, Learn from your mistakes. And so much more.

It all sounds simple, but the course gave me huge confidence and I suppose indirectly made me want to act years later. Most of all, I recognised the most invidious offence for any advocate

- an inability to be heard. Audibility and absolute clarity is utterly essential. You must speak up and project. Mumbling is out.

So why is there not much more basic training in Public Speaking in university, office and Inn of Court? Search me. But take my tip, find a good drama school or course and and enrol part-time. You are on your way to gaining a perceptible advantage over others. Speak up and win. And always use that ability when you read written statements, where your clarity and careful phrasing must. hold the attention of the jury.

# 3. Preparation and Chronologies

The new brief has arrived. Clear your desk of any other loose papers and start putting it into a usable form. In a criminal case, first strip out and file the Depositions, having removed the irrelevant documentation. In a large case, have the Interviews in a separate file. Then create a Miscellaneous file for your Instructions or Case Summary, and other papers that you must have to hand, such as medical reports. At the back, file letters to and from your instructing solicitors in chronological order. Create a special file for Disclosed Material. A further one for the Proof of the Defendant and any witnesses in support. That will leave a pile of mixed information which, having looked at briefly, can be bundled up and put aside.

The point, of course, is to divide and rule. That is how I do it, but you can find your own way of classifying the material into a form that is easily accessible and put aside that which really does not matter.

## Chronologies

I have come to realize that chronologies are an essential part of every case you undertake. It is my first act of preparation, made so simple by voice activation.

1. Create a three column Table in Word

On the left, put in the date: next the key information: next the page number or source of the material - third column can be dispensed with if you are in a hurry.

2. Press the Sort button and print it off.

In a big case, I have revised and reprinted this key document up to a dozen times as the case progressed, but this is certainly not necessary for you. Just create for your own purposes a working document that you can trust. Don't show it to the lay client, although of course it will help you when you take instructions in conference. It will help you agree a working chronology for the Court or jury with your opponent. It will be invaluable if for some reason there is a long delay in the case and you want to refresh your memory months later. And by doing the work. you will be on top of your brief, better equipped than your opponent and sometimes even the Judge.

A final word about **voice activation**. It is astonishingly useful for advocates and I do not understand today, when it really works, why more of them do not use it. Just dictate clearly and at a reasonable speed.

# 4. Opening and Closing Speeches

By opening speeches, in most cases I speak of opening for a plaintiff or opening the prosecution in a criminal case. Plainly different skills are necessary for judge and jury, but the fundamental principles of which I have already spoken come into play. Absolute clarity; never too long and at all times seek to carry your audience with you, which means engaging with them.

But probably your early experience will be prosecuting, so long as that continues to be possible. Far better that there should be a continuing professional working partnership with the Crown Prosecution Service than a total monopoly.

If you are in the Magistrates' Court, for goodness sake don't talk down to the bench. If you are in the Crown Court, prepare a clear-cut summary of the allegation and an outline of the key witnesses which support the allegation. You are discouraged today from talking about the Law, beyond perhaps the burden of proof.

But remember the huge initial advantage that a good opening gives the prosecution. You are setting the scene and telling the tale. In a fraud case, if you can get their attention at the outset, then the chances are that the jury are yours for the rest of the case. So do not make your recital of the facts so prosaic that it loses the attention of your audience. You must hold their attention and if your speeches are rambling, casual and matter-of-fact, they will not be impressed.

So when opening a case, think of a simple phrase right at the beginning which will catch their attention. It is, as it were, your own headline, although not crafted by you specifically to catch the attention of the press.

"Members of the jury we say that the defendant in this case on March 30th of this year killed his wife in the kitchen of their home. He stabbed her several times and she died where she fell."

Your own case may lack such potentially dramatic material, but you can still find a good opening sentence. Incidentally, be careful not to use crude phrases simply to make an unworthy headline. Too many references to Robin Hood in a burglary case debases the coinage

Also please avoid handing out the indictment on a pedestrian fashion at the opening of your speech. Keep any documents or documents until you have gained their initial attention. The bundle will be crucial and you will have prepared it so that all the photographs face the same way, avoiding the jury having to keep turning it from side to side. A good bundle should tell a story, so make sure it is in a chronological order with a clear readable index at the front.

## Defence Opening Speech

Today you may have the opportunity to state your case immediately after the opening. But the old way is better: if you are calling a witness in addition to your client in a criminal case, you are entitled also to open it.

Now many advocates never exercise this right. Personally I think they are mistaken. There is a great deal to be said for a short defence opening, before you call your client. For one thing, you are helping to change the atmosphere in court. By speaking, as inevitably you will, about the burden of proof, you are bringing home to the jury that they have only heard one side of it and this is the defendant's opportunity to explain what he says happened. Then summarise very shortly what you know he is going to say.

One reason why, understandably, advocates are wary of a defence opening is that the client when he gives evidence, will not live up to the advance publicity! Then make the opening short. You will find that if you craft it carefully, you will have the jury's attention and you will have given the defendant a reasonable platform from which to begin. And why not - particularly when later, you won't be able to hold his hand in cross-examination!

## Closing Speech

For many people this is what advocacy is all about: the direct appeal to a jury which cannot be interrupted, providing you state the evidence correctly.

When you are **prosecuting**, bear in mind the virtues of a firm, fair presentation. It is a terrible mistake to over-prosecute and particularly to make an inflammatory final speech. You should try to be concise and clear and seek to close down in advance all the key defence points, so far as you can do that on the evidence.

**Structure** again is very important. It is likely that you will have to deal with a prosecution witness who has either failed to come up to proof or who has deviated in a way that has caused you some embarrassment. You must confess and avoid concisely. Accept in other words that that witness did not advance matters but, on the other hand, there is a whole body of other evidence which establishes guilt.

Try to summarize all the issues chronologically and aim for devastating clarity. Try to think of the very best point in your case and leave it to the end. Having made it in outline, then develop it - but do not repeat it. The jury should feel when you sit down that the picture of guilt that you have painted is overwhelming. Further, that as the prosecutor, you has been patently fair in pointing that out. Juries appreciate fairness far more than advocates realize.

And so to **Defence Final Speeches.**

There are advocates who write out or have a very good idea of their final speech almost as soon as they have read the brief. An exaggeration perhaps, but certainly you will have formed a view of its shape fairly early, subject to the performance of the Defendant in the box.

One consequence of that is that your key cross examinations will be shaped with that final address firmly in mind. You know the need to combat the crucial evidence against you and you have to foresee how you are going to limit the damage.

I divide the evidence into **chapters** and usually tell the jury what the chapters will be in advance. That way you guarantee their attention and make it easier for them to follow your arguments. However many advocates prefer a free-flowing, more seamless approach which, however, will have been meticulously prepared.

Again, confessing and avoiding the key points against you will be an important aspect of the speech. Sometimes a simple chronology will be one of your early chapters. But ultimately you will turn to the burden of proof, in one form or another.

The heart of your speech is naked, albeit concealed persuasion. The is a matter of tone as well as evidence. As if you are voicing the hidden reservations of the jury, but without being aggressive or strident about it. But you must, repeat must hold their attention throughout to the best of your ability. Particularly that idiot in the back row who has shown disinterst or worse throughout the whole case. That involves the use of plain compelling English and a structure which is easy to follow.

I cannot emphasise how important it is that you should prepare the last few sentences of your speech. That is what you are leaving with the jury. Make it memorable if you can. Always thank them quietly at the end.

# 5. Examination in Chief and Re-Examination

This is fast becoming a neglected art. The ability to lead witnesses through their evidence by showing them their statement at the beginning may suggest that a lazy advocate need do little more than putting words into witnesses' mouths. Nothing is further from the truth. From the beginning, you should learn the art of asking the right question to persuade a witness to give his or her account in their own words. That means you must prepare every single witness that you call in Court.

Incidentally, I include in that preparation the statements that you are going to read. When reading to a jury, spot the difficult words in advance: check the pronunciation: speak up and do not rush. Nothing is more annoying than casual turgid reading at speed of agreed statements to a jury. It is evidence and you want them to understand its significance by reading well and clearly.

But back to Examination in Chief. You will be permitted to lead a few introductory questions to set the scene. With children, usually it will be in the form of a pre-recorded interview. But where a child does give evidence live, develop the art of easing them gently into the distressing evidence that they are going to have to give, but do not talk down to them. However, once you come to the meat of the statement, do not ever - and I mean ever - allow yourself to put the substance of the accusation into the witness's mouth by leading it. Not only will it attract an explosion from your opponent, but you will anger the judge. All of us realise that that sort of evidence is far less valuable than evidence that has come from the witness, however distressed that witness may be.

Now I certainly agree there will be times in your career when that is extremely difficult to do. All of us have had a witness who is so utterly distressed by their surroundings and by what has happened to them or what they have seen - that they simply cannot begin to get the words out clearly. You must be sensitive and be seen to be sensitive. Ask for a break if you think that will help.

Never bully a witness and certainly not your own. And take them as close as you can to the key issue which they alone must tell: for example, lack of consent in a rape case. Then they must say what happened with as much detail as they can bring themselves to say: you must not lead it.

I want to tell you about a great advocate in the West Country who had a brilliant technique in chief. He knew the proof inside out. He barely looked at the witness statement. He engaged the witness with his eyes and he eased out their account. It was a triumph of personality over technique. I do not pretend that you should start in that way, but if you can achieve a rapport with your witnesses, you are a long way to becoming a good advocate.

Bear in mind however that although the jury expects you to be sympathetic and polite to your witnesses, it will become uncomfortable if you are seen to help them too much. Plainly that can only benefit the cross examiner who follows you. I try to become almost invisible, once the witness is beginning to tell their story.

So examination in chief is an exercise in suppressing your enthusiasm and intervening as little as possible. If you do it well, you will win your cases, time and again.

## Hostile Witness

It happens. The animus of the your witness towards you plainly going beyond a lapse of memory. Try not to make the application until it is absolutely obvious. It is not something you want to do, because of the direction that will follow in the Summing Up, nullifying its evidential effect. My advice is that you then should put their statement to them more in sorrow than in anger and get through the process as soon as possible. Don't try to milk it because it is lazy, unattractive advocacy.

## Re-Examination

Here I want to betray a prejudice. Nothing annoys me more than advocates who lead in re-examination. It is a form of unlicensed cheating. The cross-examiner has made ground and the only way you seek to controvert it is by putting words into the witness's mouth. Don't do it. *Ever*. It is second-class advocacy and the fact that you see it happening all the time is no reason for you to do it.

However there is one qualification. Plainly, you can lead in some circumstances to clarify an answer that a witness has already given in cross-examination. Of course, you cannot introduce new material without leave of the court.

The rule is often said to be - don't re-examine unless it is absolutely necessary. True. But I have seen very skilful re-examinations which are absolutely devastating. So that it is a skill well worth acquiring.

I can't leave the subject without warning you about that nightmare moment when your client has appeared to admit the offence in cross-examination and you have to frame questions which are not leading in re-examination to try to rescue the position.

Everybody will be watching to see that you don't cheat by gross Leading. The only advice is that it may be your client did not intend to go as far in cross-examination as he did: so taking him back over the territory may, to some extent, allow him to go back to his original position. But if the admission in cross-examination had been unequivocal, it is far better to ask the judge for a few minutes and then tender your client strong advice.

Finally, I strongly encourage young advocate to go into cours specifically to watch really experienced advocates draw out frightened witnesses, without putting words into their  mouths. After a bit, you should realise that they are really building a relationship of trust with the witness, whilst at the same time, letting their own input become more and more unobtrusive. Their questions become shorter as the witness thrives. But in that apparently unselfish exercise, they are also building great credibility with the judge and jury. They are sending a coded message: you can trust me to do this fairly and skilfully - so that this witness speaks true. And the tone also of those short questions will have brought the witness safely up to proof.

# 6. Cross Examination

I will not pretend that Cross Examination is either easy or easily practised. In a sense, you will only get better by doing it. It is the very heart of advocacy and there are a few golden rules. I think the most important one is **keep it tight.** That really has two meanings.

First, put your client's case as shortly, clearly and concisely as possible and then leave it. Do not allow greater damage by giving a witness a further opportunity to expand by unnecessary questioning.

Second, it means that, as far as possible, you should try to keep control of the witness whom you are cross-examining. By that, I mean that as the questioner, you should be in the driving seat and by the precision of your questions, keep the witness to your chosen territory.

That, of course, is easier said than done. All advocates will come across a witness who, for one reason or another, runs away with the cross-examination and seemingly scores points at the time. That is the reason why cross-examination should be tight. However you can control the danger of that to some extent by the manner and the tone of your questioning.

That brings me to the second golden rule, expressed in the truism that **the art of cross-examination is not the art of examining crossly.**

It is a huge mistake to inject a degree of scorn or passion into your questions in the hope that that technique will fool your tribunal, be they judge or jury. Rudeness never pays. Discourtesy should be avoided. That is particularly true with distinguished medical witnesses. The days of savaging distinguished professional witnesses are almost over. But that does not mean that you should allow your cross-examination to degenerate into a discursive aimless chat with the witness. Keep your temper and to an extent, keep your distance.

The third rule, perhaps underpinning all others, is that you must **prepare your cross-examination meticulously.** You do need to think, so far as you can anticipate it, of the worst answer that the witness might give and think how you are going to follow up their answer.

You do need to have a structure to any cross-examination, ideally one which takes advances your case. Fundamental to your preparation is what I will call the bare minimum: <u>the essential part of your defence</u> which must be clear by your questions.

Sometimes that can be achieved at a very early stage and then left in order to turn to more profitable and less controversial territory. Such a cross-examination may not appear to be a dramatic exercise at all, but will be no less effective. In other cases you inch cautiously towards your ultimate issue. I have in mind the cross-examination of expert witnesses where putting a bald proposition too early can have devastating consequences.

The fourth rule is probably the best known. **Never ask a question,** it is said, **to which you do not know the answer already.**

Now I would qualify that rule, although this is not advice for the absolute beginner. Never ask a question unless you have a *very good idea* of what the answer is likely to be. In other words, there are times when you may feel that you can take a calculated risk. Perhaps the body language of the witness or a stray unexpected answer has provided a basis for you to take that risk. Perhaps the witness is not as hostile towards your client as you had feared.

That said, the rule is a good one. Prosecuting or Defending, you are not there to take wild risks with your instructions on a have-a-go basis. You are there to put your client's case clearly and escape with as little damage as possible.

Beyond those four rules, there is one indefinable matter which is very difficult to explain and which you will only appreciate after you have been cross-examining for a while. Something in the air which you detect and can use. Sometimes you will sense a line of cross-examination which you had not planned at all. And pursuing it carefully, suddenly the atmosphere changes in court. You have managed to pick out something which was worrying the judge or jury and by careful questions you have introduced an important and new element.

Now the cynic might call it fishing successfully. I prefer to think of it as an increased sensitivity which comes in time and which, once you experience it, will give you a huge satisfaction if you harvest it successfully.

Lastly, the visceral but concealed arts of persuasion, principally **variation of tone and pace**. I cannot teach this on paper. You have to experience for yourself the satisfaction of that better answer achieved by the gentler way of testing a particularly tricky piece of evidence,

So those are some of the basic principles. There is still a great deal to be said for buying old copies of the Notable British Trials series and reading them carefully to appreciate skilful cross-examination of another age. Or if you have the chance, go and see those advocates at the very top of their profession whom you will have learnt are successful cross-examiners. Time well spent, I suggest.

# 7. Prosecution and Defence Advocacy Tips in Rape cases

*Expanded from a Western Circuit seminar*

## Introduction

Life has changed dramatically in the conduct in court of sex cases. You will be well skilled in the gateways to the admission of Bad Character. You will know of toolkits, tagged questions and the use of Intermediaries. The starting point now for any advocate conducting sex cases is the **Advocates Gateway**. You *must* consult it. I seek a different role here: practical advice which runs alongside that fundamental legal guidance. That was the purpose of the seminar summarized below.

It was always going to be difficult to condense advocacy tips into 12 points, as I had intended. But I am very grateful to the experienced advocates who have helped me with this extended selection for this seminar. They include Susan Evans, Charlie Gabb, Ian Fenny and Louise Sweet, who all have a great deal of valuable experience in these cases.

## Prosecution

(1) See every complainant beforehand [and where required, in other non-sexual cases] to explain, reassure and undertake to

protect from unfair questions. So from the outset, present a human face.


## Example of approach:

First sit down beside them with your wig off. My name is John Doe - and I realise that you must be feeling very nervous. Perhaps I can help. I won't talk about the evidence, but I can explain shortly the way the trial will go...

Now, when you give evidence, one thing I can promise is that if you are treated unfairly by <u>anybody,</u> I shall object. So you're not going to be bullied or harassed or questioned over and over again on the same subject. But on the other hand, you understand that the defence have every right to put their questions properly and my simple advice is just to listen carefully to every question and answer it truthfully. You are not on trial and frankly it is not as you see it on TV.

You can't be pressed about something you don't know about, so if you don't know the answer, just say so. So remember if at any time you don't understand or don't know - say so. Remember that if things overwhelm you and you really need a break, then be quite sure that the Judge will let you have one.

<u>Note:</u> As a prosecutor, you may have to make the fundamental decision whether the DVD interview should be played or whether the witness should be called live. Of course, that course may be more effective to capture the essence of the allegation. This decision should be done in consultation with

the witness and the officer in the case. There is no simple answer to this, but you will have a gut instinct, having seen the complainant.

(2) Ask the complainant to describe as best they can what they felt, smelt, and/or heard during the incident.

(3) Allow the victim to explain why they acted in a manner that may seem irrational. But do not acknowledge specifically that it is irrational: bear in mind the Judge's later direction that all witnesses react differently. But you should anticipate where the weaknesses in your case may be. If necessary, be prepared to acknowledge flaws when you open your case, if only to lessen their impact at a later stage.

e.g. she didn't run out of the flat when he went to the lavatory, but the Prosecution say that she was so terrified by that stage that she should not be blamed or diminished in their eyes for not acting rationally.

Or - she didn't report it immediately because she feared what others might think of her

Or - She washed herself immediately afterwards because she said that she felt dirty. You may understand such a reaction.

(4) In the final speech, polarise:

"One conclusion is unavoidable on these facts: one side or the other must have been lying. There can be no middle ground: no other explanation."

(5) Protect the victim (and the Prosecution case) from the juries' own ignorance or misconception. Most think penetration of a vagina or anus (in context of rape) must leave some damage. Often it doesn't. Try and reduce the lack of any medical evidence to an admission that it neither supports or undermines the prosecution case.

(6) Emphasise these crimes are committed in private, so corroborative evidence is highly unlikely. Just as it is obvious that people have sex in private consensually, so it is unlikely that a man who is acting without consent does so in front of an audience.

(7) An effective and fully prepared cross examination of the Defendant is vital. It is the precursor to your speech. Indeed a good tip is to cross-examine with your final speech firmly in mind. The Defendant will not admit the offence, but he may behave as a man capable of committing the offence.

(8) In opening, it is important to stress to the jury that they are likely to be asked to recall a great deal of detailed evidence and that they may find that their memory of the complainant dims over the days of the trial. To help them in their final task, they may want to make a note of how the complainant struck them, Any points of her evidence that impressed them one way or the other. If the central point of the defence is fabrication, they may want to ask themselves the question every now and then during the course of her evidence "Is this person or child telling me the truth".

(9) It is important to prepare the jury for the format of a pre-recorded interview with a child if a substantial amount of "rapport" goes on at the start. Tell them that there will be (however many minutes) of initial chat.

(10) In a case involving a family, it will help to prepare a family tree with dates of birth. Get this agreed.

Note: Just as in a murder case, maps, plans and photos help the jury and bring the case to life. A photo of where the scene of the assault is essential for this purpose. A photograph of a child at the age when the assault is said to have occurred can be devastating,

(11) In all cases, but especially historical abuse, try to agree certain dates with the defence to enable you to give the jury the beginnings of a chronology - to which they can add as the evidence comes out. Producing a really good chronology will win you credit with the jury and will help you with your final speech.

(12) Practical steps: make sure that you are in a position to advise the Judge of lunchtime arrangements to ensure no contact between defendant and complainant. If concerned, ask for the Defendant to remain in company of solicitor or within the precincts.

# Defence

Note: You are entitled to go to see the complainant with the prosecution. That can help to take the temperature out of a difficult case, as the understanding is reached that both counsel have a job to do - to test the evidence for the jury to decide.

(1) When testing Credibility, never allege Motive unless it is absolutely clear. If it is necessary, leave it to the end of cross examination, put it shortly and sit down.

(2) Look for and identify what is odd, quirky or unusual in a complainant's account. Say to the jury: of course, make allowances for the fact that people react differently. But look for the detail where it is "very odd indeed" from a common sense point of view.

Example: where two people smoke a cigarette together after an alleged rape. It *may* be thought to be inconsistent behaviour.

(3) Be very familiar with the complainant's statement and/or DVD interview, in order to put inconsistencies. Special care is needed with a video interview to make sure that your "inconsistency" is not in fact dealt with at another point of the interview. For DVDs can disjointed and out of chronology.

Note: Be similarly familiar with the **background material.** This is where you may be able to find previous inconsistent statements or a steady "improvement" of the account being given that may suggest that there has been exaggeration or lies. It is very important to prepare a full Defence Case Statement looking for this material (or if you are prosecuting – for consistency at every stage) You should look for

a) The family liaison log

b) Notebooks of officers who attend

c) Any complaint made to the medical professionals

d) Any third party material - such as school records or social service records, where that is potentially important

e) Who the initial complaints are made to – this may be to persons in authority who have already asked questions or "tested the account." Remember this may mean the witness has had a chance to think of answers.

(4) Crystalline clarity in cross-examination. This should be done in a topic order that ensures that you are both clear and fair to the witness. You will be badly judged if you appear to be confusing the witness, even if inadvertently.

(5) Never ever demean a complainant, beyond the necessary and proper putting of your case. Avoid the dramatic assertion – 'You're lying about that' for the more courteous and effective– 'I do suggest that on that point you are not right/correct.'

Remember the *one point* anticipated by complainants is that they have been lying and making up an allegation. Understandably that suggestion, which is your case, is going to distress them, sometimes considerably. So courtesy and fairness is absolutely imperative.

(6) Have ready some "safe" topics to revert to - if the complainant looks as if she is about to become distressed. Then go back to the point that was causing distress, after she has had a few minutes to calm down.

(7) Frankly, it should rarely be necessary to go through the sexual events in minute detail in cross-examination. By going through this aspect in cross-examination, it serves to re-enforce the complaint and is likely to fill any gaps or explain any oddities. Put your case on the sexual aspect as concisely as possible – and leave it.

(8) If dealing with a complex case with many aspects, it is better to ask the Judge to allow you a few minutes to consult with your client at the end of your cross-examination to ensure that you have put all that you need to - than to risk the return of an emotional complainant later in the case.


## Recent Complaint Witnesses

Consider whether they need to be called at all, unless there are obvious inconsistencies or facts to be obtained.

(9) The paramount need for a detailed Preparation of Cross-examination of the complainant to prevent all repetition, minimise differences and to put your client's case once.

No matter how complex the case, you should be able to deal with the cross-examination in one to one and a half hours maximum. The longer the complainant is in front of the jury, the more the jury will begin to empathise with her and feel sympathy for her. With a child, you should complete your cross-examination in far less time.

<u>Note</u>: there is no obligation at all to put the dafter parts of one's instructions, which are a sideshow to their principal case. That applies particularly to suggestions that young witnesses have in some way invited the sexual conduct alleged to be criminal.

(10) Final Speech:

1. Make the point that proving a positive is easy: but it is impossible to prove a negative, namely that a sexual incident, the subject of the charge, did not occur.

2. Warn the jury of the danger of allowing emotion to influence their decisions. They must take an analytical approach.

3. Deal with the evidence in a realistic way. For example, these days, juries are not surprised if children do not make an immediate complaint to a parent.

4. In an appropriate case, say that a verdict of not guilty does not mean that they are saying that the complainant is a liar.

(11) Try hard to make your client likeable, in the face of strong evidence to the contrary!

(12) Make the very best of Character evidence. Call some individuals if you can. It goes a long way to improving the "feel" of the defence case, particularly if your client has failed to shine in evidence.

So much for respective approaches. Now, for both sides, the elephant in the room.

## Consent or the perception of Consent

This is the key issue in a high percentage of rape cases. Both advocates must understand precisely the developing law and then be able to capture it in pithy, jury friendly language. That includes the ability to spell out exactly how **Drink** consumed may impact in law on the defence being advanced. You must choose your own words, but the following examples, on either side, may figure in your final speeches.

Members of the jury

1. You should not interpret the silence or lack of objection by the complainant as an indication that she gave her real consent here…

2. The complainant has accepted that she had so much to drink that she does not have a clear memory of exactly what happened to her. That does not mean in law or on the facts that she *must* be taken to have consented to sex with the Defendant.

Alternatively

3. Bad sex is not in itself rape.

4. You may think that the complainant regretted later having had sex with the Defendant. That does not mean that she did not consent at the time that it took place.

## Final Advice

It is stating the obvious that Cross-examination in all sexual cases of is an increasingly sensitive subject and that our professional skills on both sides are under critical public examination. But done well, we can gain respect, independently of the result. Above all, try to do your job without making the ordeal for the witness one whit worse than they fear. It can be done. Good luck!

# 8. Expert Evidence

## I have decided to divide
## this section into three parts.

*'May it please you My Lord, the next witness is a consultant psychiatrist,' - moving on to Medical examiners and then Cross examination of Expert Witnesses.*

Without depressing you too much, that chapter will be the longest and I will invite the old hands present to share their own experiences at the end. So again I want to pitch this topic to help the less experienced advocates who are here.

There are of course a number of other expert witnesses in rape and other serious sexual offences. But underlying *all* these topics is the need for **detailed preparation** and knowing when to stop. The more serious point is this: the status which expert witnesses carry in the eyes of the jury. It used to be said of the most famous pathologists that their word was law and therein lay the certainty of the hangman's noose after conviction of murder.

It is still true that expert witnesses at the top of their profession carry with them into court an authority that makes it essential that, prosecuting or defending, you do not take unnecessary risks. So anybody who wishes to make the best use of a witness that they are calling - or do necessary damage to an expert witness they are cross-examining - should make it their business to understand as far as possible the medicine behind the opinion - even if it be very temporary knowledge.

That is why I have decided to start with **Psychiatrists**, who perhaps are more familiar in family courts, but may well feature in an expert capacity on questions short of intent in sexual cases. The short point is that you must master their language and understand their concepts. Sitting in mental health tribunals, we are given a training publication called *Psychiatry without Tears*. The object is for the lawyers and lay members to have an accurate guide to psychiatric concepts and conditions, in order to understand the reports in mental hospitals of responsible clinicians.

Now precisely the same guide is needed potentially for the advocate, except that you must find it out for yourself. You need to understand the differences, for example, between paranoid schizophrenia, bipolar disorder and borderline personality disorder. You need to understand that psychiatrists work on the basis of an international classification of conditions, which I assure you is pretty hard reading once you have found it. You could do worse than google the specific condition mentioned in the psychiatrist's report, not for the elegant purpose of demonstrating the weaknesses of the conclusions but simply to be able to keep up intelligently with the language.

If you do not make an effort to understand the language fully, take it from me the moment will come in cross-examination when you will be shown to be the rank amateur that in fact you are. Psychiatrists have a disarming habit of leaning over the side of the witness box, lowering their horn-rimmed glasses and gently correcting your lay language as you examine their concepts.

I do not want anyone to think that I have anything less than enormous respect for good consultant psychiatrists. In fact, now that I understand more fully their working methods and their ability to answer their question **why** rather than our question **how**, I am frequently in awe of their intellectual analysis, dedication, diagnosis and treatment. So should you be.

Two weeks ago, defending in a diminished responsibility case, two outstanding psychiatrists held the stage and commanded real respect. One of them, Dr Richard Babcock for the Crown, is the doctor upon whom the series Cracker was based, although anyone looking less like Robbie Coltrane let alone Hagrid - would be hard to imagine. The point that I want to make about in was his presentational skills and how Prosecuting counsel literally simply let him speak without interruption. It was very good advocacy.

So Dr Babcock did indeed put his papers down, look across at the jury and talk to them without a trace of condescension and have their complete attention. But under that genial and persuasive manner was a steely intellect able to call on massive experience of murder to distinguish our case from others where perhaps diminished responsibility had had more productive soil from which to grow.

The lesson for the advocate is that if you have a first-class witness who is at home in the witness box, then you need a very light rein indeed.

But to achieve that degree of unassisted fluency, it must have been necessary to have taken Dr Babcock through his opinion with care and to have agreed to reduce the base material to that which really mattered. You should take the same approach in your preparation of similar witnesses.

## Pathologist and Medical examiners.

A little advice in dealing with that level of expertise in court. I seek always to spend time with pathologists in order to make absolutely sure that they will be on script and not advance without warning a theory as to, for example, the mechanics of the killing. Similarly, it is necessary to know in advance exactly how far the medical examiner is likely to go when pressed or challenged in cross-examination on obvious topics.

I am not for one moment talking about coaching an expert witness. That is impermissible. I mean understanding an expert witness and the relative strength of his or her opinion. So of course, I am speaking also of a pre-trial conference with the expert.

But once you have established the level of their expertise and refined in your mind the accuracy of their examination - using your advocate's eye as to their likely impact on the jury – you need to decide just how much of their examination is strictly necessary for the proof of your case. Forensic medical examination may carry with it a great deal more detail than you require.

Precisely the same point may be made in murder cases, where some parts of the pathologist's examination are, in fact, completely irrelevant. The stab wounds yes, of course. But those parts of the anatomy and inner organs untouched by the violent death have no part to play in the case and it is completely unnecessary to bring it to the jury's attention.

So when you have the results of the forensic medical examination in a full report, you should have the courage to use your judgement as to just how much of it is really necessary to prove your case. As with much good advocacy, less may be more.

That links with the other great skill which is so difficult for a beginner to do, namely to leave out a less important piece of evidence deliberately - so that a jury can make the connection for itself. If that sounds dangerous to you, the older advocates in this room will know exactly what I mean.

Now with those principles in mind, can I just spend a few minutes on the **cross-examination of expert witnesses**, bearing in mind the title of this seminar. Let me go back to psychiatrists and another lesson or two - as it happens from the same case a couple of weeks ago.

Every professional psychiatrist knows that their Achilles heel is the accuracy of information on which their opinion is based. They will have the depositions: they will have interviewed the witness or the defendant, but they may not necessarily have heard all the tapes or seen all the DVDs. Equally they are probably much too busy to have sat through the trial and absorbed the evidence.

So if you are calling that psychiatrist, you need to give him or her a crash course on the evidence that has arisen in order to limit embarrassment in cross-examination. That may very well include additional evidence that has been read to the jury. So don't let your witness going to court unprepared - because the base material has not been available or there have been important changes during the case.

If you are cross examining however, then it is perfectly legitimate to examine the sources of that information, in order to see whether it is soundly based. At the same time you should remember that you are dealing with professional witnesses and not with professional fraudsters.

So the robust language of cross-examination may need some modification when dealing with most professional witnesses. The days of the ritual savagery of a defence psychiatrist and distinguished professional are very nearly over, even if that may disappoint a few hardy advocates at the back of the hall.

The second point to bear in mind, particularly with a psychiatrist, is the extent to which their opinion is based on the defendant's own account in their professional examination of him. And here I want to sound a warning note to those who think that there must be always a good opportunity to make a cheap point in front of the jury.

"Why Doctor, you have no idea whether the defendant was telling you the truth, have you?"

No, but they do have a lifetime of distinguishing between genuine psychosis and malingerers. They are often very good at explaining the difference. So your crowd-pleasing question may produce an explanation and reasoning which damages your case.

The last point I want to make about psychiatrists is make sure when the defendant has been in custody, that you pay meticulous attention to the prison medical notes, once you have obtained them, to see the extent to which they have been absorbed by the psychiatrist whom you are questioning. More importantly still, whether prison psychiatric evidence clashes with the opinion being given. You should know that in the prison medical wing where a defendant is being kept and assessed, daily and sometimes twice-daily reports are being made on his state of mind. So you can trace for example the difference between depression and psychosis where that is shown in the notes.

I am conscious that there are other expert witnesses who may be called in rape cases that I have not considered. For example, DNA evidence where the odds are 1,000,000 to 1 the wrong way! Beyond suggesting that you should examine with great care the possibility of contamination which does still happen, I accept that the only way to deal with witnesses as deadly as that is to get them out of the witness box as soon as possible.

Finally I would like to tell you a little story about DNA evidence which may not have a great deal to do with this seminar, but does show that you should not lose heart. Some years ago I was asked to advise in a murder case in the Werst Country where the defendant had been interviewed five times but had never been charged, because there was no forensic evidence. Then, in prison for some other offence, he had boasted of the killing to a few criminals with appalling records, whose word was not likely to be believed on oath.

I advised that whilst there was a prima facie case, I was not optimistic that we could or would succeed. Two weeks before the hearing I had a telephone call from a very excited police officer.

"Mr Pascoe, you'll never guess what has happened.!

We have re-examined the ropes that were used to bind the victim before she was killed and guess what - thanks to the very latest mitochondrial DNA analysis, we can prove that he did it."

And he had done. A weak case had become a very strong one. And even though the prisoners were still not very good witnesses, armed with this tremendous bonus, we got home.

Good luck with your examination and cross-examination of expert witnesses. But in a word, handle with care!

# 9. Submissions

If at all possible, prepare clear concise skeleton arguments with relevant extracts from authority. Think consciously of the manner of presentation. A small font and a smudged photocopy will simply irritate the Court. So your skeleton arguments should be as professionally presented as you can make them.

Once it is plain that the Court has read the skeleton argument, there is no need at all to repeat it, word for word. A good technique is to pick the best point and develop that one alone. Judges do not wish to hear jury speeches wrapped up as submissions. The best submissions are clothed in detached dispassionate language.

After your opponent has replied, normally the Judge will ask you if you have anything else to say. It is a tricky moment. Obviously you must not repeat all that you said the first time. But if you seize on the weakest part of your opponent's response, it is just possible that you may win at the last hurdle. So keep it brief.

# 10. Pleas in Mitigation

Despite your best endeavours, your client has been convicted and things are not looking too good. But a good plea is still possible. Here are the rules.

First **Know the Law**. Easily said, I know, but as sentencing becomes more difficult, advocates are now required to share the load with the judge. That includes a working knowledge of sentencing guidelines where that is appropriate.

Second, a good plea is about **judgement of possibilities**. So don't ask for the moon when the case is so serious that a custodial sentence is inevitable and the only issue is the length of time to be served. Try to tailor your submissions to a possible and realistic disposal.

Third, begin by making brief submissions on the **facts** of the case. Try not to go on about how serious the cases: that may be self-evident. Instead pick on safe points, which may be about the relative seriousness of the offence and, for example, legitimate provocation which may have occurred during the incident.

Fourth -and obviously - use the positive features of the **Pre-sentence Report**. But if it contains a damaging risk assessment, you should try to qualify it if possible by evidence which has been before the Court.

Fifth, make the best use you can of any **References** which you possess. I take the business of constructing a plea in mitigation very seriously and encourage these letters to be obtained well before the hearing. They should not, of course, ever comment on the accusation that the defendant faces. Comment like -

'I don't believe he is capable of doing that' are completely counter-productive. But a well-presented readable file of letters from responsible members of the community, employers and some relatives can have a significant effect in mitigation.

Whether or not to call a **Character Witness** is sometimes a difficult judgement. Good judges will "take it from you" rather than require a distressed wife to have to give evidence. But there are cases where a close family relative can make a significant difference. Try to avoid character evidence which is likely to be over-emotional, because quite simply it may not work. A good employer, however, who has been prepared to come to court or an army officer standing by a member of his platoon can be very valuable.

Finally, make your plea in **direct and restrained terms**. Indeed that is the best advice I can give. It will be more effective if it is detached, so that the mitigation speaks for itself. It is also much easier for the sentencing Judge to assess carefully, rather than an overt appeal to emotion. Emotion has its place but it should be carefully concealed in calm persuasive language. One of the skills of Sir Norman Birkett KC was to put the emotion in the middle of his sentences but then end them in a quieter, less pejorative form. That is very difficult to do until you have confidence in your speaking abilities. For the time being, keep emotion firmly at bay.

# 11. In The Cells

The purpose of this chapter is to give a little practical advice before and after sentence in criminal proceedings. I am lucky enough to have conducted my cases almost invariably with a solicitor or representative present and later with a junior. In other words, an independent recollection if things go wrong and the client starts making allegations about his counsel. You will not always have that advantage and frequently be obliged to take instructions alone.

I cannot emphasise too much how important it is to have decided before your conference with the client exactly what information you need. There will be gaps in your own instructions which you can fill at short notice, as well as question marks or downright lies to be explored. But you are not there to re-check everything in the proof. You haven't got the time and difficult clients can vary their accounts from day to day. By concentrating on the key points, you are in effect bulking up your cross examination to concentrate on what really matters.

Mr Pascoe, what is my likely sentence? Of course, you answer cautiously and never promise a result. But you must be on top of the Sentencing Guidelines to be able to give a range of possible sentences. That means you must also prepare the client for the worst, particularly if of previous good character or has not served a custodial sentence. I usually say whatever happens, I'll come down and we will discuss it together. A promise which of course which you must keep.

But what if the worst has happened? A sentence at the top end? I always refuse to give immediate advice on the prospects of an appeal against conviction or sentence. I do point out where the judge may have made a mistake, but you must never gave false hope. On sentence, I usually say that I want to look again at the latest authorities on the particular facts and if they wish and fill in the form in prison, we will provide an advice in more writing in 14 days. But it is a terrible mistake to empathise with the client and build up his hopes, particularly as that will be relayed to his immediate family and potentially mislead and distress them even more. Far better to be sympathetic but detached. Just seek to be professional and clinical in the careful advice which you give.

Finally, the nightmare scenario when you are criticised - or worse, abused on your own with the client. Do not hesitate to withdraw, gracefully if possible, from any case where you are being criticised by angry or perhaps disturbed clients. In the event of a row, you may even have to consider asking a nearby prison officer to make a note of what was being shouted. Make a contemporaneous note yourself as soon as possible. Incidentally, you should always try to establish a good informal relationship with prison officers and a little levity does no harm.

# 12. Advocacy on Appeal

Like many advocates, my experiences in the Court of Appeal have been mixed, to put it mildly. I managed once to make one of the mildest and most courteous of Judges shout at me, causing me to try out anger management techniques at short notice. Other outings have been more productive, usually when I managed to keep it short. Clearly some greater expertise is necessary.

So I have prepared this chapter first on the basis of an outstanding talk given to the Western Circuit by Sir John Royce, former Presiding Judge and one time Circuit Leader. Second, a Bar Council workshop, which I reviewed for Counsel Magazine and introduced by Lord Justice Potter and Mr Justice Hunt. As a preface, let me stress how important it is that would-be advocates spent time at the back of Appeal Courts to pick up the atmosphere, speed of proceedings and the and the need to read the Court, particularly when they indicate that they have the point…

The day has dawned. Will your skeleton argument stand up to analysis? How long should you be? What is the court like and should you adapt your style to their flavour? In the words of an old story, the Reading factor, things seemed fine when you got on the train to London from the West Country. The you look again at your Grounds of Appeal. But by the time you have reached Reading, a sinking feeling has developed and you begin to wonder why on earth you put that point in the

Grounds? By London, your Appeal is going to be so much shorter...

1. The starting point is the preparation of your Grounds of Appeal. You must be absolutely ruthless in paring them down to the minimum. Leave out those half points, often minor issues of fact. They will haunt you before an unimpressed Court and they damage your credibility. That said, flesh out those good grounds with necessary detail. It will have been the first document that the Court will have read on the night before the hearing.

2. Make the document attractive to read. So avoid a small font. Use short numbered consecutive paragraphs, avoiding para 1.1. etc and leave space for the Court to annotate. Use names in shorthand rather than Appellant or Respondent.

3. Try to begin with a single arresting sentence. So for example, on an Appeal against Conviction, you can say 'My Lords, I have leave to argue this point'. Say it clearly and with confidence. The Court really wants to know as soon as possible what was wrong with the judgement being appealed. Attractive presentation of the issues engenders the feelgood factor. Bear in mind that the Court will have discussed that point beforehand and will have a preliminary view of it.

4. Avoid lengthy quotations from authorities. Select first your strongest point and build on it. Above all, perhaps, keep it short. Melford Stevenson J, told that he had been upheld on appeal, memorably said – 'Well, I still think I was right'.

5. Quote your strongest case at the highest judicial level.

6. Go for cases reported in the last two or three years.

7. On Appeals against Sentence, avoid citing A-G references because there is double jeopardy there.

8. In the seminar, the late and much admired Mr Justice (James) Hunt, clearly disturbed by indifferent advocacy in his last three weeks in the Court of Appeal Crim Div, gave equally pungent advice. It needs to be shouted from the rooftops, because it is universal from Judges hearing appeals. **Presentation, presentation, presentation is everything**. Advocates addressing their feet are known backstage as noddy dogs and memorably he demonstrated that appalling but sadly frequent habit. Use lecterns, he urged, to look at the Court and hold their attention. He quoted hilariously a judicial aside – 'The wonderful thing about being mediocre is that he is always at his best.'

9. Finally, remember that the 4th member of the Court is the single Judge who has given you leave. The worse question you can be asked is – What are you asking for? That means you have failed abjectly to get it across. But take comfort: keeping it short and tight is the best way of all.

# 13. A Glimpse of
# Lord Norman Birkett KC

## [taken in part from *Sweet Reason,* my play about his life]

Norman - later Lord Birkett, Kings Counsel, was one of the greatest advocates of the 20th century. Every student of advocacy would do well to read about him and if possible, hunt down old recordings on You Tube or elsewhere. A famous question in cross examination is worth remembering.

## Birkett

What is the co-efficient of linear expansion of brass? You know, it would be very strange if in the years to come, they remember me for that single opening question. I was prosecuting in a case called Rouse, a most dreadful murder. The Defence called a gentleman as a so-called expert and in cross examination, I simply wanted to test his expertise. Happily for me, he did not know the answer!

I have often been asked what I would have done if he had answered correctly. Probably I would have asked about another non-ferrous metal…provided that I also knew the answer! Never Ask A Question if you don't! You see, Advocacy has been my life. And of course, watching Lancashire play cricket!

**NP** Silver tongued with a most beguiling voice, Norman Birkett was hugely admired, not as a lawyer but as the ultimate advocate. A born actor, a gift of lucid exposition, a superb sense of timing and rhetoric, and a flair for achieving dramatic effects by deliberate understatement.

Two days before he died and then a Liberal peer in the House of Lords, he helped to stop Manchester Corporation from draining his beloved Ullswater of yet more water sought for municipal purposes. What follows is an edited summary of that magnificent speech. The old advocate still remembered how to do it.

# Birkett

The Chairman of the Waterworks has given an undertaking, I understand, that they will seek no more from Ullswater. It is like the extempore speech of which Lord Hewart used to speak; it is not worth the paper it is written on. The Manchester Corporation can no more bind its successors than anybody else can. Manchester is saying now:

"Give us the powers, let us do this, and the amenities of Lakeland and of Ullswater will be quite untouched and quite undiminished" There was a phrase used by the noble Viscount, the Leader of the House, the other day in a debate. "By their fruits ye shall know them". We have only to look at Thirlmere and Haweswater as they are to-day. Both lovely lakes have been *murdered*. They are now dead water reservoirs: no human life; sterile shores. And they come to this House with this Bill now and say, "We are only going to destroy a valley.

The question for Your Lordships is a simple one. At this moment, February, 1962, shall the Manchester Corporation be permitted to invade Lakeland for the third time, to impound its waters, to pour them into its aqueducts, - or not?

And the great overriding principle - are we going to allow this in a National Park? Set up so that the scenic beauty should be preserved and that their enjoyment should be for all people in all times. And to say "There have been many invasions there. Here is one more", is a *pitiful* argument.

Before I sit down I shall make one plea that your Lordships will assert that Parliament has said that these areas, few though they be, in our land shall be preserved inviolateI know perfectly well what people feel about it. We are unaccustomed to use words such as "This precious stone set in the silver sea." We think it, but we rarely say it.

I am greatly tempted when it comes to defending the beauty of the English Lakelands—so small, so lovely, so vulnerable upon that account—to call to aid the great Wordsworth, the great men who have lived there and who have had the power to set down upon the printed pad what scenic beauty can mean to the individual life and to the life of the nation.

So far from saying in this House - "It has been done many times. Let it be done once more", surely the argument should be, "It has been too many times already; do not let us add to it".

My Lords, I suppose that to-day we have a House which is as full as any I have had the privilege of addressing, and I suppose this would be the moment for what I would call my peroration. I leave it on one side; I do not feel equal to a peroration on a theme like this at this moment, and will content myself by saying this. Your Lordships will have a great opportunity this evening when the Division is taken to vindicate the right of the House to say on any measure such as this: thus far and no farther. Go away. Come again another day, if you will. But in the meantime, do that which ought to have been done before. Produce the hydrological data on which the House can come to a proper decision. Until that is done, you have no right whatever to invade the sanctity of a National Park."

**NP** The House supported him and two days later, he died. In the words of his wife – on the crest of a wave. Advocacy still matters.

# 14. 'Friends, Romans and countrymen...'

There is no better illustration of the skills of advocacy outside the law courts than the funeral speech that Shakespeare gives to Mark Antony after the killing of Julius Caesar. Whether Shakespeare worked in a lawyer's office in the missing eight years of his life remains a matter of speculation. Somehow he managed to glean many of the key facets of persuasion and demonstrate them in an unforgettable and glittering form. Rarely was that better demonstrated than in the early outstanding production at the Bridge Theatre, London, with David Morrissey as Mark Antony, which for me was one of the highlights of a lifetime loving good theatre.

I have included the speech without further comment, save to invite the readers to discover for themselves the arts and artifices which permeate our craft.

**ANTONY**
Friends, Romans, countrymen, lend me your ears;
I come to bury Caesar, not to praise him.
The evil that men do lives after them;
The good is oft interred with their bones;
So let it be with Caesar. The noble Brutus
Hath told you Caesar was ambitious:
If it were so, it was a grievous fault,
And grievously hath Caesar answer'd it.
Here, under leave of Brutus and the rest--

For Brutus is an honourable man;
So are they all, all honourable men--
Come I to speak in Caesar's funeral.
He was my friend, faithful and just to me:
But Brutus says he was ambitious;
And Brutus is an honourable man.
He hath brought many captives home to Rome
Whose ransoms did the general coffers fill:
Did this in Caesar seem ambitious?
When that the poor have cried, Caesar hath wept:
Ambition should be made of sterner stuff:
Yet Brutus says he was ambitious;
And Brutus is an honourable man.
You all did see that on the Lupercal
I thrice presented him a kingly crown,
Which he did thrice refuse: was this ambition?
Yet Brutus says he was ambitious;
And, sure, he is an honourable man.
I speak not to disprove what Brutus spoke,
But here I am to speak what I do know.
You all did love him once, not without cause:
What cause withholds you then, to mourn for him?
O judgment! thou art fled to brutish beasts,
And men have lost their reason. Bear with me;
My heart is in the coffin there with Caesar,
And I must pause till it come back to me.

**First Citizen**
Methinks there is much reason in his sayings.

**Second Citizen**

If thou consider rightly of the matter,
Caesar has had great wrong.

**Third Citizen**

Has he, masters?
I fear there will a worse come in his place.

**Fourth Citizen**

Mark'd ye his words? He would not take the crown;
Therefore 'tis certain he was not ambitious.

**First Citizen**

If it be found so, some will dear abide it.

**Second Citizen**

Poor soul! his eyes are red as fire with weeping.

**Third Citizen**

There's not a nobler man in Rome than Antony.

**Fourth Citizen**

Now mark him, he begins again to speak.

**ANTONY**

But yesterday the word of Caesar might
Have stood against the world; now lies he there.
And none so poor to do him reverence.
O masters, if I were disposed to stir
Your hearts and minds to mutiny and rage,

I should do Brutus wrong, and Cassius wrong,
Who, you all know, are honourable men:
I will not do them wrong; I rather choose
To wrong the dead, to wrong myself and you,
Than I will wrong such honourable men.
But here's a parchment with the seal of Caesar;
I found it in his closet, 'tis his will:
Let but the commons hear this testament--
Which, pardon me, I do not mean to read--
And they would go and kiss dead Caesar's wounds
And dip their napkins in his sacred blood,
Yea, beg a hair of him for memory,
And, dying, mention it within their wills,
Bequeathing it as a rich legacy
Unto their issue.

**Fourth Citizen**
We'll hear the will: read it, Mark Antony.

**All**
The will, the will! we will hear Caesar's will.

**ANTONY**
Have patience, gentle friends, I must not read it;
It is not meet you know how Caesar loved you.
You are not wood, you are not stones, but men;
And, being men, bearing the will of Caesar,
It will inflame you, it will make you mad:
'Tis good you know not that you are his heirs;
For, if you should, O, what would come of it!

**Fourth Citizen**

Read the will; we'll hear it, Antony;
You shall read us the will, Caesar's will.

**ANTONY**

Will you be patient? will you stay awhile?
I have o'ershot myself to tell you of it:
I fear I wrong the honourable men
Whose daggers have stabb'd Caesar; I do fear it.

**Fourth Citizen**

They were traitors: honourable men!

**All**

The will! the testament!

**Second Citizen**

They were villains, murderers: the will! read the will.

**ANTONY**

You will compel me, then, to read the will?
Then make a ring about the corpse of Caesar,
And let me show you him that made the will.
Shall I descend? and will you give me leave?

**Several Citizens**

Come down.

**Second Citizen**

Descend.

**Third Citizen**
You shall have leave.

*ANTONY comes down*

**Fourth Citizen**
A ring; stand round.

**First Citizen**
Stand from the hearse, stand from the body.

**Second Citizen**
Room for Antony, most noble Antony.

**ANTONY**
Nay, press not so upon me; stand far off.

**Several Citizens**
Stand back; room; bear back.

**ANTONY**
If you have tears, prepare to shed them now.
You all do know this mantle: I remember
The first time ever Caesar put it on;
'Twas on a summer's evening, in his tent,
That day he overcame the Nervii:
Look, in this place ran Cassius' dagger through:
See what a rent the envious Casca made:
Through this the well-beloved Brutus stabb'd;
And as he pluck'd his cursed steel away,

Mark how the blood of Caesar follow'd it,
As rushing out of doors, to be resolved
If Brutus so unkindly knock'd, or no;
For Brutus, as you know, was Caesar's angel:
Judge, O you gods, how dearly Caesar loved him!
This was the most unkindest cut of all;
For when the noble Caesar saw him stab,
Ingratitude, more strong than traitors' arms,
Quite vanquish'd him: then burst his mighty heart;
And, in his mantle muffling up his face,
Even at the base of Pompey's statua,
Which all the while ran blood, great Caesar fell.
O, what a fall was there, my countrymen!
Then I, and you, and all of us fell down,
Whilst bloody treason flourish'd over us.
O, now you weep; and, I perceive, you feel
The dint of pity: these are gracious drops.
Kind souls, what, weep you when you but behold
Our Caesar's vesture wounded? Look you here,
Here is himself, marr'd, as you see, with traitors.

**First Citizen**
O piteous spectacle!

**Second Citizen**
O noble Caesar!

**Third Citizen**
O woful day!

**Fourth Citizen**
O traitors, villains!

**First Citizen**
O most bloody sight!

**Second Citizen**
We will be revenged.

**All**
Revenge! About! Seek! Burn! Fire! Kill! Slay!
Let not a traitor live!

**ANTONY**
Stay, countrymen.

**First Citizen**
Peace there! hear the noble Antony.

**Second Citizen**
We'll hear him, we'll follow him, we'll die with him.

**ANTONY**
Good friends, sweet friends, let me not stir you up
To such a sudden flood of mutiny.
They that have done this deed are honourable:
What private griefs they have, alas, I know not,
That made them do it: they are wise and honourable,
And will, no doubt, with reasons answer you.
I come not, friends, to steal away your hearts:

I am no orator, as Brutus is;
But, as you know me all, a plain blunt man,
That love my friend; and that they know full well
That gave me public leave to speak of him:
For I have neither wit, nor words, nor worth,
Action, nor utterance, nor the power of speech,
To stir men's blood: I only speak right on;
I tell you that which you yourselves do know;
Show you sweet Caesar's wounds, poor poor dumb mouths,
And bid them speak for me: but were I Brutus,
And Brutus Antony, there were an Antony
Would ruffle up your spirits and put a tongue
In every wound of Caesar that should move
The stones of Rome to rise and mutiny.

**All**
We'll mutiny.

**First Citizen**
We'll burn the house of Brutus.

**Third Citizen**
Away, then! come, seek the conspirators.

**ANTONY**
Yet hear me, countrymen; yet hear me speak.

**All**
Peace, ho! Hear Antony. Most noble Antony!

**ANTONY**

Why, friends, you go to do you know not what:
Wherein hath Caesar thus deserved your loves?
Alas, you know not: I must tell you then:
You have forgot the will I told you of.

**All**

Most true. The will! Let's stay and hear the will.

**ANTONY**

Here is the will, and under Caesar's seal.
To every Roman citizen he gives,
To every several man, seventy-five drachmas.

**Second Citizen**

Most noble Caesar! We'll revenge his death.

**Third Citizen**

O royal Caesar!

**ANTONY**

Hear me with patience.

**All**

Peace, ho!

**ANTONY**

Moreover, he hath left you all his walks,
His private arbours and new-planted orchards,
On this side Tiber; he hath left them you,

And to your heirs for ever, common pleasures,
To walk abroad, and recreate yourselves.
Here was a Caesar! when comes such another?

**First Citizen**
Never, never. Come, away, away!
We'll burn his body in the holy place,
And with the brands fire the traitors' houses.
Take up the body.

**Second Citizen**
Go fetch fire.

**Third Citizen**
Pluck down benches.

**Fourth Citizen**
Pluck down forms, windows, any thing.

*Exeunt Citizens with the body*

**ANTONY**
Now let it work. Mischief, thou art afoot,
Take thou what course thou wilt!

# 15. Reflections

I am writing this on the way down from Edinburgh, after an unexpected change of venue in the middle of a regulatory hearing. This time the pleasure has been listening, as a legal assessor, to two very different and able advocates doing their stuff in surroundings far more prosaic than a Crown Court. But this has been a stimulus for a reflective and wider look at advocacy. It is not always hearts and flowers before a bemused jury.

I want to return to the analogy that the true advocate is one who can put it across better than the closest of the Defendant's friends. Someone, that is, who knows the Defendant, warts and all and has the ability, at least in theory, to present him or her in a very attractive light. You have to be better than that. Every time. Take it from me, it is worth the effort. I don't regret the effort for a second.

And therein, sometimes, lies a touch of magic and a good place to end. Set out to carry the Court, sustain the defendant and win the jury. But work at your craft every single day. Advocates, to adapt Alan Bennett from The History Boys, just want to pass it on.

Which reminds me - where is that next case that the clerks mentioned? Well that sounds fun…

**Nigel Pascoe QC**          **June 2018**

# About the Author

Nigel Pascoe QC took silk in 1988. He is a specialist practitioner in Jury advocacy, principally in Crime. He was a Recorder of the Crown Court between 1979 and 2013 with a ticket to sit in serious sexual cases for over seven years. He also sat for twelve years as a President of Mental Health Tribunals, sitting in restricted cases and regularly in Broadmoor Hospital. He conducted an enquiry into the conduct of a former MP. More recently he has been appointed as a Legal Assessor to the Nursing and Midwifery Council.

Nigel Pascoe is the senior member of Chambers and has been one of the top jury advocates in the country since taking Silk in 1988. Formerly Leader of the Western Circuit and Chairman of the Bar Public Affairs Committee. he has prosecuted and defended equally in high-profile murder cases. To date, he has been briefed in well over 120 murder cases, inclung many of the major Circuit cases of the last 25 years. He s a Bencher of the Inner Temple.

Among his reported cases are *R v Hyde, Sussex and Collins*, which is the leading authority on the foresight of intention in murder and *R v Cairns*, concerning disclosure of defence statements and the prosecution's discretion to call a witness who is not wholly credible. He provided the Archbold commentary on the case. He was Chairman of the Board of Counsel magazine, remaining on the Board and was the founder and presenter of All England Quarterly Law Reports, as well as writing and broadcasting on a range of legal issues.

He is a former Chairman of the Bar Public Affairs Committee, a BBC media trainer and a contributor to the NSPCC video on the cross-examination of children. He has trained other barristers on the Western Circuit, particularly in cross-examination in serious sexual cases and also on the nature of Mental Health proceedings.

Nigel Pascoe once again appeared in Chambers and Partners in the 2012, 2013, 2014, 2015, 2016, 2017 and 2018 editions, including – *"another former leader of the Western Circuit and has a reputation as a very good jury advocate, who is very charming and persuasive... and very accomplished."* Also - *"renowned amongst commentators for his charismatic court room manner."* He is also recommended in the latest edition of the Legal 500 as Leading Silk within Crime.

Nigel Pascoe has a corresponding career as an actor and playwright, notably with a one-man show –*The Trial of Penn and Mead (Old Bailey 1670)* which has had nearly 100 performances and which he has taken with his wife Elizabeth to different parts of the world.

32990293R00046

Printed in Great Britain
by Amazon